Pope Francis
Speaks to Families

WORDS OF

Joy

AND

Life

the**WORD**
among us®
press

Published by The Word Among Us Press
7115 Guilford Road
Frederick, Maryland 21704
www.wau.org

19 18 17 16 15   1 2 3 4 5
ISBN: 978-1-59325-272-4
eISBN: 978-1-59325-467-4

Pope Francis's homilies and addresses are taken from the Vatican
translation and can be found on the Vatican website,
www.vatican.va. Used with permission of
Libreria Editrice Vaticana.

Cover design by Koechel Peterson & Associates
Cover image: Pope Francis hugs a child as he arrives to
lead the weekly audience in St. Peter's Square at the Vatican,
June 19, 2013. Reuters/Stefano Rellandini

Library of Congress Control Number: 2015934604

CONTENTS

Thinkstock Photos

INTRODUCTION

Few public figures in modern times have grasped the imagination of the world as Pope Francis has. His charm, his sincerity, and his ability to express profound concepts in a down-to-earth way have won him the respect and attention of millions. This book draws from the rich vein of wisdom that he has offered to the modern family.

The excerpts you will find here are taken from many different occasions and settings but consistently echo the themes that we have come to expect of Pope Francis. Rich messages of forgiveness, caring, and love are delivered with a practicality and gentle humor. He has words for those in all stages of family life—those engaged to be married, husbands and wives, parents, grandparents, young people, and children.

The contemporary social landscape has changed. "We see the family and marriage undergoing a deep inner crisis in the countries of the Western world," Pope Francis has observed. This makes the family "a new mission field for the Church." The Holy

Father calls on families to be witnesses to the world of fidelity, purity, and humble service. Above all, he says, we need God—"his help, his strength, his blessing, his mercy, his forgiveness."

We hope that you and your family will experience great blessings from the words in this book. It is not all comfortable reading—following God's plan for your family can be challenging at times. But the wisdom it conveys is essential if our families are to become the strong building blocks that the Church is built upon. May the Lord give you and your family—the domestic church—all the grace and strength you need to be witnesses of God's love and mercy to the world.

The Word Among Us Press

Prayer for the Synod on the Family

Jesus, Mary and Joseph,
in you we contemplate
the splendor of true love,
to you we turn with trust.

Holy Family of Nazareth,
grant that our families too
may be places of communion and prayer,
authentic schools of the Gospel,
and small domestic Churches.

Holy Family of Nazareth,
may families never again
experience violence, rejection, and division:
may all who have been hurt or scandalized
find ready comfort and healing.

Holy Family of Nazareth,
may the approaching Synod of Bishops
make us once more mindful

of the sacredness and inviolability of the family,
and its beauty in God's plan.

Jesus, Mary, and Joseph,
graciously hear our prayer.

CHAPTER

I

MARRIAGE

Marriage: The Image of God

This sacrament [Matrimony] leads us to the heart of God's design, which is a plan for a covenant with his people, with us all, a plan for communion. At the beginning of the Book of Genesis, the first book of the Bible, at the culmination of the creation account, it says: "God created man in his own image, in the image of God he created him; male and female he created them. . . . Therefore a man leaves his father and his mother and cleaves to his wife, and they become one flesh" (Genesis 1:27; 2:24).

The image of God is the married couple: the man and the woman; not only the man, not only the woman, but both of them together. This is the image of God: love, God's covenant with us, is represented in that covenant between man and woman. And this is very beautiful! We are created in order to love, as a reflection of God and his love. And in the marital union, man and woman fulfill this vocation through their mutual reciprocity and their full and definitive communion of life.

—GENERAL AUDIENCE,
ST. PETER'S SQUARE, APRIL 2, 2014

Two Become One

When a man and woman celebrate the Sacrament of Matrimony, God, as it were, "is mirrored" in them; he impresses in them his own features and the indelible character of his love. Marriage is the icon of God's love for us. Indeed, God is communion too: the three Persons of the Father, the Son, and the Holy Spirit live eternally in perfect unity. And this is precisely the mystery of matrimony: God makes of the two spouses one single life. The Bible uses a powerful expression and says "one flesh," so intimate is the union between man and woman in marriage. And this is precisely the mystery of marriage: the love of God which is reflected in the couple that decides to live together. Therefore a man leaves his home, the home of his parents, and goes to live with his wife and unites himself so strongly to her that the two become—the Bible says—one flesh.

—GENERAL AUDIENCE, ST. PETER'S SQUARE,
APRIL 2, 2014

Hand in Hand

Those who celebrate the sacrament [of Matrimony] say, "I promise to be true to you, in joy and in sadness, in sickness and in health; I will love you and honor you all the days of my life." At that moment, the couple does not know what will happen, nor what joys and pains await them. They are setting out, like Abraham, on a journey together. And that is what marriage is! Setting out and walking together, hand in hand, putting yourselves in the Lord's powerful hands. Hand in hand, always and for the rest of your lives. And do not pay attention to this makeshift culture, which can shatter our lives.

—ADDRESS TO THE PILGRIMAGE OF FAMILIES,
ST. PETER'S SQUARE, OCTOBER 26, 2013

Ever More a Woman, Ever a More Man

The love of Christ, which has blessed and sanctified the union of husband and wife, is able to sustain their love and to renew it when, humanly speaking, it becomes lost, wounded, or worn out. The love of Christ can restore to spouses the joy of journeying together. This is what marriage is all about: man and woman walking together, wherein the husband helps his wife to become ever more a woman, and wherein the woman has the task of helping her husband to become ever more a man. This is the task that you both share. "I love you, and for this love I help you to become ever more a woman"; "I love you, and for this love I help you to become ever more a man."

—Homily at Mass for the Rite of Marriage, St. Peter's Square, September 14, 2014

Marriage Is a Celebration

Marriage is a celebration—a Christian celebration, not a worldly feast! The Gospel of John points to the most profound reason for joy on that day: do you remember the miracle at the wedding in Cana? At a certain point, there was no more wine and the celebration seemed to be ruined. Imagine drinking tea at the end of a celebration! No, it's not good! There is no party without wine! At Mary's suggestion, in that moment Jesus reveals himself for the first time and gives a sign: he transforms water into wine, thus saving the wedding feast.

What happened in Cana two thousand years ago happens today at every wedding celebration: that which makes your wedding full and profoundly true will be the presence of the Lord who reveals himself and gives his grace. It is his presence that offers the "good wine"; he is the secret to full joy, that which truly warms the heart. It is the presence of Jesus at the celebration. May it be a beautiful celebration, but with Jesus!

—ADDRESS TO ENGAGED COUPLES,
ST. PETER'S SQUARE, FEBRUARY 14, 2014

Be Revolutionaries!

In these days, as you reflect on the complementarity between man and woman, I urge you to emphasize yet another truth about marriage: that the permanent commitment to solidarity, fidelity, and fruitful love responds to the deepest longings of the human heart. Let us think especially of the young people who represent our future: it is important that they should not let the harmful mentality of the temporary affect them, but rather that they be revolutionaries with the courage to seek strong and lasting love; in other words, to go against the current: this must be done.

—HUMANUM COLLOQUIUM, ROME,
NOVEMBER 17, 2014

Love Forever

It's important to ask yourself if it is possible to love each other "forever." This is a question that must be asked: is it possible to love "forever"? Today so many people are afraid of making definitive decisions. One boy said to his bishop, "I want to become a priest, but only for ten years." He was afraid of a definitive choice. But that is a general fear that comes from our culture. To make life decisions seems impossible. Today everything changes so quickly; nothing lasts long. And this mentality leads many who are preparing for marriage to say, "We are together as long as the love lasts," and then? All the best and see you later . . . and so ends the marriage.

But what do we mean by "love"? Is it only a feeling, a psychophysical state? Certainly, if that is it, then we cannot build on anything solid. But if, instead, love is a relationship, then it is a reality that grows, and we can also say by way of example that it is built up like a home. And a home is built together, not alone! To build something here means to foster and aid growth.

Dear engaged couples, you are preparing to grow together, to build this home, to live together forever. You do not want to found it on the sand of sentiments, which come and go, but on the rock of true love, the love that comes from God. The family is born from this plan of love; it wants to grow just as a home is built, as a place of affection, of help, of hope, of support. As the love of God is stable and forever, so too should we want the love on which a family is based to be stable and forever. Please, we mustn't let ourselves be overcome by the "culture of the provisory"! Today this culture invades us all, this culture of the temporary. This is not right!

—ADDRESS TO ENGAGED COUPLES,
ST. PETER'S SQUARE, FEBRUARY 14, 2014

We Need the Grace of the Sacrament

With trust in God's faithfulness, everything can be faced responsibly and without fear. Christian spouses are not naïve; they know life's problems and temptations. But they are not afraid to be responsible before God and before society. They do not run away; they do not hide; they do not shirk the mission of forming a family and bringing children into the world.

"But today, Father, it is difficult." . . . Of course it is difficult! That is why we need the grace, the grace that comes from the sacrament! The sacraments are not decorations in life—what a beautiful marriage, what a beautiful ceremony, what a beautiful banquet. . . . But that is not the Sacrament of Marriage. That is a decoration! Grace is not given to decorate life but rather to make us strong in life, giving us courage to go forward! And without isolating oneself but always staying together. Christians celebrate the Sacrament of Marriage because they know they need it! They need it to stay together and to carry out their mission as parents. "In joy and in sadness, in sickness and in health."

This is what the spouses say to one another during the celebration of the sacrament, and in their marriage they pray with one another and with the community. Why? Because it is helpful to do so? No! They do so because they need to, for the long journey they are making together: it is a long journey, not for a brief spell but for an entire life! And they need Jesus' help to walk beside one another in trust, to accept one another each day, and daily to forgive one another.

—ADDRESS TO THE PILGRIMAGE OF FAMILIES,
ST. PETER'S SQUARE, OCTOBER 26, 2013

A Craftsman's Task

Marriage is . . . an everyday task, I could say a craftsman's task, a goldsmith's work, because the husband has the duty of making the wife more of a woman, and the wife has the duty of making the husband more of a man. Growing also in humanity, as man and woman. And this you do together. This is called growing together. This does not come out of thin air! The Lord blesses it, but it comes from your hands, from your attitudes, from your way of loving each other. To make us grow!

Always act so that the other may grow. Work at this. And thus, I don't know, I am thinking of you that one day you will walk along the streets of your town and the people will say, "Look at that beautiful woman, so strong! . . . With the husband that she has, it's understandable!" And to you, too: "Look at him and how he is! . . . With the wife he has, I can understand why!" It's this, reaching this point: making one another grow together, one another. And the children will have the inheritance of having a father and a mother who grew together, making each other—one another—more of a man and more of a woman!

—Address to Engaged Couples,
St. Peter's Square, February 14, 2014

There Will Be Crosses!

It is normal for husband and wife to argue—it's normal. It always happens. But my advice is this: never let the day end without having first made peace. Never! A small gesture is sufficient. Thus the journey may continue. Marriage is a symbol of life, real life—it is not "fiction"! It is the sacrament of the love of Christ and the Church, a love which finds its proof and guarantee in the cross. My desire for you is that you have a good journey, a fruitful one, growing in love. I wish you happiness. There will be crosses! But the Lord is always there to help us move forward.

—HOMILY AT MASS FOR THE RITE OF MARRIAGE,
ST. PETER'S SQUARE, SEPTEMBER 14, 2014

Love Is Stronger Than the Moment

It is true that there are so many difficulties in married life, so many, when there is insufficient work or money, when the children have problems. So much to contend with. And many times the husband and wife become a little fractious and argue between themselves. They argue, this is how it is; there is always arguing in marriage, sometimes the plates even fly. Yet we must not become saddened by this; this is the human condition. The secret is that love is stronger than the moment when there is arguing, and therefore I always advise spouses: do not let a day when you have argued end without making peace. Always! And to make peace, it isn't necessary to call the United Nations to come to the house and make peace. A little gesture is sufficient, a caress, and then let it be! Until tomorrow! And tomorrow, begin again. And this is life, carrying on, carrying on with courage and the desire to live together. And this is truly great; it is beautiful!

—GENERAL AUDIENCE,
ST. PETER'S SQUARE, APRIL 2, 2014

Give Us This Day Our Daily Love

A marriage is not successful just because it endures; quality is important. To stay together and to know how to love one another forever is the challenge for Christian couples. What comes to mind is the miracle of the multiplication of the loaves: for you, too, the Lord can multiply your love and give it to you fresh and good each day. He has an infinite reserve! He gives you the love that stands at the foundation of your union, and each day he renews and strengthens it. And he makes it ever greater when the family grows with children. On this journey prayer is important; it is necessary, always: he for her, she for him, and both together.

Ask Jesus to multiply your love. In the prayer of the Our Father, we say, "Give us this day our daily bread." Spouses can also learn to pray like this: "Lord, give us this day our daily love," for the daily love of spouses is bread, the true bread of the soul; what sustains them in going forward.

And the prayer: can we practice to see if we know how to say it? "Lord, give us this day our daily love." All together! [Couples]: "Lord, give us this day our daily love." One more time! [Couples]: "Lord give us this day our daily love." This is the prayer for engaged couples and spouses. Teach us to love one another, to will good to the other! The more you trust in him, the more your love will be "forever," able to be renewed, and it will conquer every difficulty.

—ADDRESS TO ENGAGED COUPLES,
ST. PETER'S SQUARE, FEBRUARY 14, 2014

Three Magic Words for Married Life

Married life is such a beautiful thing, and we must treasure it always, treasure the children. . . . There are three words that always need to be said, three words that need to be said at home: may I, thank you, and sorry.

The three magic words. May I, so as not to be intrusive in the life of the spouses. May I, but how does it seem to you? May I, please allow me. Thank you, to thank one's spouse: thank you for what you did for me, thank you for this. That beauty of giving thanks! And since we all make mistakes, that other word, which is a bit hard to say but which needs to be said: sorry. Please, thank you, and sorry.

With these three words, with the prayer of the husband for the wife and vice versa, by always making peace before the day comes to an end, marriage will go forward. The three magic words, prayer, and always making peace.

—GENERAL AUDIENCE,
ST. PETER'S SQUARE, APRIL 2, 2014

Rules for the Journey: "May I?"

"Can I, may I?" This is the polite request to enter the life of another with respect and care. One should learn how to ask: "May I do this?" "Would you like for us to do this?" "Should we take up this initiative, to educate our children in this way?" "Do you want to go out tonight?" In short, to ask permission means to know how to enter with courtesy into the lives of others. . . .

It's not easy, not easy at all. Sometimes, however, manners are used in a heavy way, like hiking boots! True love does not impose itself harshly and aggressively. In the *Fioretti* [Little Flowers] of St. Francis, we find this expression: "For know, dear brother, that courtesy is one of the attributes of God, . . . for courtesy is the sister of charity, it extinguisheth hatred and kindleth love" (chapter 37). Yes, courtesy kindles love. And today in our families, in our world, which is frequently violent and arrogant, there is so much need for courtesy. And this can begin at home.

—ADDRESS TO ENGAGED COUPLES,
ST. PETER'S SQUARE, FEBRUARY 14, 2014

Rules for the Journey: "Thank You"

Thank you." It seems so easy to say these words, but we know that it is not. But it is important! We teach it to children, but then we ourselves forget it! Gratitude is an important sentiment! . . . An old woman once said to me in Buenos Aires, "Gratitude is a flower that grows on a noble ground." Nobility of soul is necessary so that this flower might grow.

Do you remember the Gospel of Luke? Jesus heals ten lepers and then only one returns to say thank you to Jesus. The Lord says, "And the other nine, where are they?" (cf. Luke 17:11-19). This also holds true for us: do we know how to give thanks? In your relationship, and tomorrow in married life, it is important to keep alive the awareness that the other person is a gift from God—and for the gifts of God we say thank you, we must always give thanks for them. And in this interior attitude one says "thank you" to the other for everything. It is not a kind word to use with strangers, to show you are polite. You need to know how to say thank you in order to go forward in a good way together in married life.

—ADDRESS TO ENGAGED COUPLES,
ST. PETER'S SQUARE, FEBRUARY 14, 2014

Rules for the Journey: "I'm Sorry"

In life we err frequently; we make many mistakes. We all do. . . . Perhaps not a day goes by without making some mistake. The Bible says that the just man sins seven times a day (cf. Proverbs 24:16). And thus, we make mistakes. Hence the need to use these simple words: "I'm sorry." In general, each of us is ready to accuse the other and to justify ourselves. This began with our father Adam, when God asks him, "Adam, have you eaten of the fruit?" "Me? No! It was her, she gave it to me!" (cf. Genesis 3:11-14). Accusing the other to avoid saying "I'm sorry," "Forgive me"—it's an old story! It is an instinct that stands at the origin of so many disasters. Let us learn to acknowledge our mistakes and to ask for forgiveness.

In this way, too, a Christian family grows. We all know that the perfect family does not exist, nor a perfect husband or wife . . . we won't even speak about a perfect mother-in-law. We sinners exist. Jesus, who knows us well, teaches us a secret: don't let a day end without asking forgiveness, without peace returning to our home, to our family. It is normal for husband and wife to quarrel. . . . Perhaps you were mad, perhaps plates flew, but please remember this: never let the sun go down without making peace! Never, never, never! This is a secret, a secret for maintaining love and making peace.

Pretty words are not necessary. . . . Sometimes just a simple gesture and . . . peace is made. Never let a day end . . . for if you let the day end without making peace, the next day what is inside of you is cold and hardened, and it is even more difficult to make peace. Remember: never let the sun go down without making peace! If we learn to say sorry and ask one another for forgiveness, the marriage will last and move forward. When elderly couples, celebrating fifty years together, come to audiences or Mass here at Santa Marta, I ask them, "Who supported whom?" This is beautiful! Everyone looks at each other; they look at me and say, "Both!" And this is beautiful! This is a beautiful witness!

—Address to Engaged Couples,
St. Peter's Square, February 14, 2014

Making Christ's Love Visible

St. Paul, in the Letter to the Ephesians, emphasizes that a great mystery is reflected in Christian spouses: the relationship established by Christ with the Church, a nuptial relationship (cf. 5:21-33). The Church is the bride of Christ. This is their relationship. This means that matrimony responds to a specific vocation and must be considered as a consecration (cf. *Gaudium et Spes*, 48; *Familiaris Consortio*, 56). It is a consecration: the man and woman are consecrated in their love. The spouses, in fact, by virtue of the sacrament, are invested with a true and proper mission so that starting with the simple ordinary things of life, they may make visible the love with which Christ loves his Church, by continuing to give his life for her in fidelity and service.

—GENERAL AUDIENCE,
ST. PETER'S SQUARE, APRIL 2, 2014

The Marital Bond Is Preserved through Prayer

There is a truly marvelous design inherent in the Sacrament of Matrimony! And it unfolds in the simplicity and frailty of the human condition. We are well aware of how many difficulties two spouses experience. . . . The important thing is to keep alive their bond with God, who stands as the foundation of the marital bond. And the true bond is always the Lord. When the family prays, the bond is preserved. When the husband prays for his wife and the wife prays for her husband, that bond becomes strong; one praying for the other.

—GENERAL AUDIENCE,
ST. PETER'S SQUARE, APRIL 2, 2014

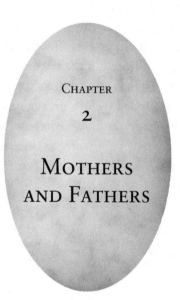

CHAPTER

2

MOTHERS
AND FATHERS

A Child Changes Your Life!

Motherhood and fatherhood are a gift of God, but to accept the gift, to be astounded by its beauty, and to make it shine in society, this is your task. Each of your children is a unique creature that will never be duplicated in the history of humanity. When one understands this, or that God wanted each one, we are astounded by how great a miracle a child is! A child changes your life! We have all seen—men, women—that when a child arrives, life changes, it is another thing. A son or daughter is a miracle that changes life.

—ADDRESS TO THE ITALIAN ASSOCIATION OF
LARGE FAMILIES, DECEMBER 28, 2014

Fathers, Be Close to Your Children

I ask for you [fathers] the grace to be ever closer to your children; allow them to grow, but be close, close! They need you, your presence, your closeness, your love. May you be for them as St. Joseph was: guardians of their growth in age, wisdom, and grace. May you guard them on their journey: be educators and walk with them. And by this closeness, you will be true educators.

—GENERAL AUDIENCE,
ST. PETER'S SQUARE, MARCH 19, 2014

A Mother Knows What's Important for Her Children

I ask myself: what does a mother do? First of all, she teaches how to walk through life; she teaches the right path to take through life; she knows how to guide her children; she always tries to point out to them the right path in life for growing up and becoming adults. And she does so with tenderness, affection, and love, even when she is trying to straighten out our path because we are going a little astray in life or are taking roads that lead to an abyss. A mother knows what's important for a child to enable him to walk the right way through life. Moreover, she did not learn it from books but from her own heart. The university of mothers is their heart! They learn there how to bring up their children. . . . A mother never teaches what is evil; she only wants the good of her children, and so does the Church.

—GENERAL AUDIENCE,
ST. PETER'S SQUARE, SEPTEMBER 18, 2013

A Mother Knows How to Balance Things

A mother . . . thinks of the health of her children, teaching them also to face the difficulties of life. You do not teach, you do not take care of health by avoiding problems, as though life were a motorway with no obstacles. The mother helps her children to see the problems of life realistically and not to get lost in them, but to confront them with courage; not to be weak, and to know how to overcome them, in a healthy balance that a mother "senses" between the area of security and the area of risk. And a mother can do this! She does not always take the child along the safe road, because in that way the child cannot develop, but neither does she leave the child only on the risky path, because that is dangerous. A mother knows how to balance things. A life without challenges does not exist, and a boy or a girl who cannot face or tackle them is a boy or girl with no backbone!

—ADDRESS AT THE RECITATION OF THE ROSARY,
PAPAL BASILICA OF ST. MARY MAJOR, MAY 4, 2013

You Are the Father!

The absent father figure in the life of little ones and young people causes gaps and wounds that may even be very serious. And, in effect, delinquency among children and adolescents can be largely attributed to this lack, to the shortage of examples and authoritative guidance in their everyday life, a shortage of closeness, a shortage of love from the father. And the feeling of orphanhood that so many young people live with is more profound than we think.

They are orphaned in the family because the father is often absent, also physically, from the home, but above all because when they are present, they do not behave like fathers. They do not converse with their children. They do not fulfill their role as educators. They do not set their children a good example with their words, principles, values, those rules of life which they need like bread. The educative quality of the time the father spends raising the child is all the more necessary when he is forced to stay away from home because of work.

Sometimes it seems that fathers don't know what their role in the family is or how to raise their children. So, in doubt, they abstain; they retreat and neglect their responsibilities, perhaps taking refuge in the unlikely relationship as "equals" with their children. It's true that you have to be a "companion" to your child, but without forgetting that you are the father! If you behave only as a peer to your child, it will do him or her no good.

—GENERAL AUDIENCE,
PAUL VI HALL, JANUARY 28, 2015

A Good Mother Helps Her Children

A mother does not stop at just giving life; with great care she helps her children grow, gives them milk, feeds them, teaches them the way of life, accompanies them always with her care, with her affection, with her love, even when they are grown up. And in this she also knows to correct them, to forgive them and understand them. She knows how to be close to them in sickness and in suffering. In a word, a good mother helps her children to come of themselves, and not to remain comfortably under her motherly wings, like a brood of chicks under the wings of the broody hen.

—GENERAL AUDIENCE,
ST. PETER'S SQUARE, SEPTEMBER 11, 2013

We Should Listen to Mothers

Perhaps mothers, ready to sacrifice so much for their children and often for others as well, ought to be listened to more. We should understand more about their daily struggle to be efficient at work and attentive and affectionate in the family; we should better grasp what they aspire to in order to express the best and most authentic fruits of their emancipation. A mother with her children always has problems, always work. I remember there were five of us children at home, and while one was doing one thing, the other wanted to do another, and our poor mama went back and forth from one's side to another, but she was happy. She gave us so much.

Mothers are the strongest antidote to the spread of self-centered individualism. "Individual" means "what cannot be divided." Mothers, instead, "divide" themselves, from the moment they bear a child to give him to the world and help him grow.

—GENERAL AUDIENCE, PAUL VI HALL, JANUARY 7, 2015

Knock at God's Heart with Prayers for Your Children

For her children, a mother is also able to ask and knock at every door, without calculation; she does so out of love. And I think of how mothers can also and especially knock at the door of God's heart! Mothers say so many prayers for their children, especially for the weaker ones, for those in the greatest need or who have gone down dangerous or erroneous paths in life.

A few weeks ago, I celebrated Mass in the Church of St Augustine, here in Rome, where the relics of St. Monica, his mother, are preserved. How many prayers that holy mother raised to God for her son, and how many tears she shed! I am thinking of you, dear mothers: how often you pray for your children, never tiring! Continue to pray and to entrust them to God; he has a great heart! Knock at God's heart with prayers for your children.

—GENERAL AUDIENCE,
ST. PETER'S SQUARE, SEPTEMBER 18, 2013

Mothers Are Not Afraid

When a child grows up, becomes an adult, he chooses his path, assumes his responsibilities, stands on his own two feet, does what he likes, and at times he can also go off course; some accident occurs. A mother has the patience to continue to accompany her children, always and in every situation. It is the force of her love that impels her; a mother can follow her children on their way with discretion and tenderness and even when they go astray, always finds a way to understand them, to be close, to help.

We—in my region—say that a mother can *"dar la cara."* What does this mean? It means that a mother can "put on a brave" for her children; in other words, she is always motivated to defend them. I am thinking of the mothers who suffer for their children in prison or in difficult situations: they do not question whether or not their children are guilty; they keep on loving them. Mothers often suffer humiliation, but they are not afraid; they never cease to give of themselves.

—GENERAL AUDIENCE,
ST. PETER'S SQUARE, SEPTEMBER 18, 2013

St. Joseph: A Model for Every Father

It would be a grave error to think that a father and mother can do nothing to form their child to grow in the grace of God. To grow in age, to grow in wisdom, and to grow in grace: this is the work Joseph did with Jesus, to help him grow in these three ways, to aid his growth.

Dear brothers and sisters, Joseph's mission is certainly unique and unrepeatable, because Jesus is absolutely unique. And yet, in his guardianship of Jesus, forming him to grow in age, wisdom, and grace, he is a model for every educator, especially every father. St. Joseph is the model of the educator and the dad, the father. I, therefore, entrust to his protection all parents, priests—who are fathers—and those who have an educational role in the Church and in society.

—GENERAL AUDIENCE,
ST. PETER'S SQUARE, MARCH 19, 2014

Not to Have Children Is a Selfish Choice

A society with a paucity of generations, which does not love being surrounded by children, which considers them above all a worry, a weight, a risk, is a depressed society. Let us consider the many societies we know here in Europe: they are depressed societies, because they do not want children, they are not having children, the birth rate does not reach one percent. Why? . . . If a family with many children is looked upon as a weight, something is wrong! The child's generation must be responsible, as the Encyclical *Humanae Vitae* of Blessed Pope Paul VI also teaches, but having many children cannot automatically be an irresponsible choice. Not to have children is a selfish choice. Life is rejuvenated and acquires energy by multiplying: it is enriched, not impoverished! Children learn to assume responsibility for their family. They mature in sharing its hardship. They grow in the appreciation of its gifts.

—GENERAL AUDIENCE,
ST. PETER'S SQUARE, FEBRUARY 11, 2015

Children Are a Gift

Children are the joy of the family and of society. They are not a question of reproductive biology, nor one of the many ways to fulfill oneself, much less a possession of their parents. . . . No. Children are a gift, they are a gift: understood? Children are a gift. Each one is unique and irreplaceable; and at the same time unmistakably linked to his or her roots. In fact, according to God's plan, being son and daughter means to carry within oneself the memory and hope of a love which was fulfilled in the very kindling of the life of another, original and new, human being. And for parents each child is original, different, diverse.

Allow me to share a family memory. I remember what my mother said about us—there were five of us—"I have five children." When they asked her, "Which one is your favorite," she answered, "I have five children, like five fingers. Should they strike this one, it hurts me; should they strike that one, it hurts me. All five hurt me. All are my children and all are different like the fingers of a hand." And this is how a family is! The children are all different, but all children.

A child is loved because he is one's child: not because he is beautiful, or because he is like this or like that; no, because he is a child! Not because he thinks as I do, or embodies my dreams. A child is a child: a life generated by us but intended for him, for his good, for the good of the family, of society, of mankind as a whole.

—General Audience,
St. Peter's Square, February 11, 2015

Fathers Must Be Present and Patient

Every family needs a father. . . . The first need . . . is precisely this: that a father be *present* in the family. That he be close to his wife, to share everything, joy and sorrow, hope and hardship. And that he be close to his children as they grow: when they play and when they strive, when they are carefree and when they are distressed, when they are talkative and when they are silent, when they are daring and when they are afraid, when they take a wrong step and when they find their path again; a father who is always present. To say "present" is not to say "controlling"! Fathers who are too controlling cancel out their children; they don't let them develop.

The Gospel speaks to us about the exemplarity of the Father who is in heaven—who alone, Jesus says, can be truly called the "good Father" (cf. Mark 10:18). Everyone knows that extraordinary parable of the "prodigal son," or better yet, of the "merciful father," which we find in the Gospel of Luke in chapter 15 (cf. 15:11-32). What dignity and what tenderness there is in the expectation of that father, who stands at the door of the house waiting for his son to return! Fathers must be patient. Often there is nothing else to do but wait; pray and wait with patience, gentleness, magnanimity, and mercy. . . .

If, then, there is someone who can fully explain the prayer of the "Our Father," taught by Jesus, it is the one who lives out paternity in the first person. Without the grace that comes from the Father who is in heaven, fathers lose courage and abandon camp. But children need to find a father waiting for them when they come home after failing. They will do everything not to admit it, not to show it, but they need it; and not to find it opens wounds in them that are difficult to heal.

—GENERAL AUDIENCE,
PAUL VI HALL, FEBRUARY 4, 2015

CHAPTER

3

FAMILY LIFE

Is There Joy in Your Family?

In the responsorial psalm, we find these words: "Let the humble hear and be glad" (34:2). The entire psalm is a hymn to the Lord, who is the source of joy and peace. What is the reason for this gladness? It is that the Lord is near; he hears the cry of the lowly and he frees them from evil. As St. Paul himself writes, "Rejoice always . . . The Lord is near" (cf. Philippians 4:4-5).

I would like to ask you all a question today. But each of you keep it in your heart and take it home. You can regard it as a kind of "homework." Only you must answer. How are things when it comes to joy at home? Is there joy in your family? You can answer this question.

Dear families, you know very well that the true joy which we experience in the family is not superficial; it does not come from material objects, from the fact that everything seems to be going well. . . . True joy comes from a profound harmony between persons, something which we all feel in our hearts and which makes us experience the beauty of togetherness, of mutual support along life's journey. But the basis of this feeling of deep joy is the presence of God, the presence of God in the family and his love, which is welcoming, merciful, and respectful towards all. And, above all, a love which is patient: patience is a virtue of God, and he teaches us how to cultivate it in family life, how to be patient, and lovingly so, with each other. To be patient among ourselves; a patient love. God alone knows how to create harmony from differences.

But if God's love is lacking, the family loses its harmony; self-centeredness prevails and joy fades. But the family which experiences the joy of faith communicates it naturally. That family is the salt of the earth and the light of the world; it is the leaven of society as a whole.

—HOMILY FOR FAMILY DAY,
ST. PETER'S SQUARE, OCTOBER 27, 2013

Welcome Jesus into Your Home

The Son of God chose to be born into a human family, in an obscure town on the periphery of the Roman Empire. Although the Gospels tell us little about the first thirty years of his life, we can imagine that Jesus led a very "normal" family life. He was raised in an atmosphere of religious devotion, he learned from the words and example of Mary and Joseph, and he grew in wisdom, age, and grace (cf. Luke 2:52). In imitation of the Holy Family, every Christian family must make a place for Jesus in its home. For it is through the love of such "normal" families that God's Son quietly comes to dwell among us, bringing salvation to our world. . . .

And this is the great mission of the family: to make room for Jesus who is coming, to welcome Jesus in the family, in each member: children, husband, wife, grandparents. . . . Jesus is there. Welcome him there, in order that he grow spiritually in the family.

GENERAL AUDIENCE,
ST. PETER'S SQUARE, DECEMBER 17, 2014

The Family Was the Path of Jesus

Jesus "was obedient to them"—that is, to Mary and Joseph (Luke 2:51). And someone might say: "But did this God, who comes to save us, waste thirty years there, in that suburban slum?" He wasted thirty years! He wanted this. Jesus' path was in that family—"and his mother kept all these things in her heart. And Jesus increased in wisdom and in stature, and in favor with God and man" (2:51-52). It does not recount miracles or healing, or preaching—he did none in that period—or of crowds flocking; in Nazareth everything seemed to happen "normally," according to the customs of a pious and hardworking Israelite family: they worked, the mother cooked, she did all the housework, ironed shirts . . . all the things mothers do. The father, a carpenter, worked, taught his son the trade. Thirty years. "But what a waste, Father!" God works in mysterious ways. But what was important there was the family! And this was not a waste!

—General Audience,
St. Peter's Square, December 17, 2014

Make Time to Rest in Prayer

Rest is so necessary for the health of our minds and bodies, and often so difficult to achieve due to the many demands placed on us. But rest is also essential for our spiritual health, so that we can hear God's voice and understand what he asks of us. Joseph was chosen by God to be the foster father of Jesus and the husband of Mary. As Christians, you too are called, like Joseph, to make a home for Jesus. To make a home for Jesus! You make a home for him in your hearts, your families, your parishes, and your communities.

To hear and accept God's call, to make a home for Jesus, you must be able to rest in the Lord. You must make time each day to rest in the Lord, to pray. To pray is to rest in the Lord. But you may say to me: "Holy Father, I know that; I want to pray, but there is so much work to do! I must care for my children; I have chores in the home; I am too tired even to sleep well." I know. This may be true, but if we do not pray, we will not know the most important thing of all: God's will for us. And for all our activity, our busyness, without prayer we will accomplish very little.

—MEETING WITH FAMILIES, MALL OF ASIA ARENA,
MANILA, JANUARY 16, 2015

The Family That Prays Together Stays Together

Don't forget: the family that prays together stays together! This is important. There we come to know God, to grow into men and women of faith, to see ourselves as members of God's greater family, the Church. In the family we learn how to love, to forgive, to be generous and open, not closed and selfish. We learn to move beyond our own needs, to encounter others and share our lives with them. That is why it is so important to pray as a family! So important! That is why families are so important in God's plan for the Church!

—MEETING WITH FAMILIES, MALL OF ASIA ARENA, MANILA, JANUARY 16, 2015

The Devil Tries to Destroy the Family

Families are the domestic church, where Jesus grows; he grows in the love of spouses, he grows in the lives of children. That is why the enemy so often attacks the family. The devil does not want the family; he tries to destroy it, to make sure that there is no love there. Married couples are sinners, like us all, but they want to go forward in faith, in fruitfulness, in their children and their children's faith. May the Lord bless families and strengthen them in this time of crisis when the devil is seeking to destroy them.

—ADDRESS TO THE CONVOCATION OF THE RENEWAL OF THE HOLY SPIRIT, OLYMPIC STADIUM, JUNE 1, 2014

Give Your Children the Word of God

God, like a good father and a good mother, wants to give good things to his children. And what is this nourishing food that God gives us? It is *his word*: his word makes us grow; it enables us to bear good fruit in life, just as the rain and snow imbue the earth, making it fruitful (cf. Isaiah 55:10-11). Likewise you, parents, and you too, godmothers and godfathers, grandparents, aunts and uncles, will help these children grow if you give them the word of God, the Gospel of Jesus. And give it also by your example! Every day, make it a habit to read a passage of the Gospel, a small one, and always carry a little Gospel with you in your pocket, in your purse, so you can read it. And this will set the example for your children, seeing dad, mom, their godparents, grandpa, grandma, aunts and uncles reading the word of God.

—HOMILY AT MASS ADMINISTERING BAPTISM,
JANUARY 11, 2015

Do We "Waste Time" with Children?

We have to ask ourselves: who are we, as we stand before the Child Jesus? Who are we, standing as we stand before today's children? Are we like Mary and Joseph, who welcomed Jesus and cared for him with the love of a father and a mother? Or are we like Herod, who wanted to eliminate him? Are we like the shepherds, who went in haste to kneel before him in worship and offer him their humble gifts? Or are we indifferent? Are we, perhaps, people who use fine and pious words, yet exploit pictures of poor children in order to make money? Are we ready to be there for children, to "waste time" with them? Are we ready to listen to them, to care for them, to pray for them and with them? Or do we ignore them because we are too caught up in our own affairs?

—HOMILY, MANGER SQUARE, BETHLEHEM,
MAY 25, 2014

Be Immersed in the Holy Spirit

Dear parents, dear godfathers and godmothers, if you want your children to become true Christians, help them to grow up "immersed" in the Holy Spirit, that is to say, in the warmth of the love of God, in the light of his Word. For this reason, do not forget to invoke the Holy Spirit often, every day. . . . We usually pray to Jesus. When we pray the Our Father, we pray to the Father. But we do not often pray to the Holy Spirit. It is very important to pray to the Holy Spirit, because he teaches us how to bring up the family, the children, so that these children may grow up in the atmosphere of the Holy Trinity. It is precisely the Spirit who leads them forward. For this reason, do not forget to invoke the Holy Spirit often, every day. You can do so, for example, with this simple prayer: "Come, Holy Spirit, fill the hearts of your faithful and kindle in them the fire of your love." You can say this prayer for your children, as well as, naturally, for yourselves!

When you recite this prayer, you feel the maternal presence of the Virgin Mary. She teaches us to pray to the Holy Spirit, and to live in accordance with the Spirit, like Jesus. May Our Lady, our Mother, always accompany the journey of your children and of your families. So be it.

—HOMILY AT MASS ADMINISTERING BAPTISM,
JANUARY 11, 2015

A Perfect Family Does Not Exist

More than anywhere else, the family is where we daily experience our own limits and those of others, the problems great and small entailed in living peacefully with others. A perfect family does not exist. We should not be fearful of imperfections, weakness, or even conflict, but rather learn how to deal with them constructively. The family, where we keep loving one another despite our limits and sins, thus becomes a school of forgiveness. Forgiveness is itself a process of communication. When contrition is expressed and accepted, it becomes possible to restore and rebuild the communication which broke down. A child who has learned in the family to listen to others, to speak respectfully, and to express his or her view without negating that of others, will be a force for dialogue and reconciliation in society.

—MESSAGE FOR THE WORLD COMMUNICATIONS DAY,
JANUARY 23, 2015

Do Not Stop Dreaming!

I am very fond of dreams in families. For nine months every mother and father dream about their baby. Am I right? [Yes!] They dream about what kind of child he or she will be. . . . You can't have a family without dreams. Once a family loses the ability to dream, children do not grow, love does not grow, life shrivels up and dies. So I ask you each evening, when you make your examination of conscience, to also ask yourselves this question: Today did I dream about my children's future? Today did I dream about the love of my husband, my wife? Did I dream about my parents and grandparents who have gone before me? Dreaming is very important. Especially dreaming in families. Do not lose this ability to dream!

How many difficulties in married life are resolved when we leave room for dreaming, when we stop a moment to think of our spouse, and we dream about the goodness present in the good things all around us.

—MEETING WITH FAMILIES, MALL OF ASIA ARENA, MANILA, JANUARY 16, 2015

Pray for Siblings at Odds

In the family . . . , how many siblings quarrel over little things, or over an inheritance, and then they no longer speak to each other, they no longer greet one another. This is terrible! Brotherhood is a great thing when we consider that all our brothers and sisters lived in the womb of the same mother for nine months, came from the mother's flesh! Brotherhood cannot be broken. Let us consider: we all know families that have divided siblings, who have quarreled; let us ask the Lord—perhaps in our family there are a few cases—to help these families to reunite their siblings, to rebuild the family. Brotherhood must not be broken, and when it breaks, what happened to Cain and Abel occurs. When the Lord asks Cain where his brother is, he replies: "I do not know, my brother does not matter to me" (cf. Genesis 4:9). This is terrible; it is a very, very painful thing to hear. In our prayers let us always pray for siblings who are at odds.

—GENERAL AUDIENCE,
ST. PETER'S SQUARE, FEBRUARY 18, 2015

Simplicity

Our gaze on the Holy Family lets us . . . be drawn into the simplicity of the life they led in Nazareth. It is an example that does our families great good, helping them increasingly to become communities of love and reconciliation, in which tenderness, mutual help, and mutual forgiveness is experienced. . . . I would also like to encourage families to become aware of the importance they have in the Church and in society. The proclamation of the Gospel, in fact, first passes through the family to reach the various spheres of daily life.

—ANGELUS,
ST. PETER'S SQUARE, DECEMBER 29, 2013

Keeping the Faith

The apostle Paul, at the end of his life, makes a final reckoning and says, "I have kept the faith" (2 Timothy 4:7). But how did he keep the faith? Not in a strong box! Nor did he hide it underground, like the somewhat lazy servant (cf. Matthew 25:17-19). St. Paul compares his life to a fight and to a race. He kept the faith because he didn't just defend it but proclaimed it, spread it, brought it to distant lands. He stood up to all those who wanted to preserve, to "embalm" the message of Christ within the limits of Palestine. That is why he made courageous decisions; he went into hostile territory; he let himself be challenged by distant peoples and different cultures; he spoke frankly and fearlessly. St. Paul kept the faith because, in the same way that he received it, he gave it away; he went out to the fringes and didn't dig himself into defensive positions.

Here, too, we can ask: how do we keep our faith as a family? Do we keep it for ourselves, in our families, as a personal treasure like a bank account, or are we able to share it by our witness, by our acceptance of others, by our openness? We all know that families, especially young families, are often "racing" from one place to another, with lots to do. But did you ever think that this "racing" could also be the race of faith? Christian families are missionary families. Yesterday in this square we heard the testimonies of missionary families. They are missionary also in everyday life, in their doing everyday things, as they bring to everything the salt and the leaven of faith! Keeping the faith in families and bringing to everyday things the salt and the leaven of faith.

—HOMILY FOR FAMILY DAY,
ST. PETER'S SQUARE, OCTOBER 27, 2013

What It Means to Pray as a Family

I would like to ask you, dear families: do you pray together from time to time as a family? Some of you do, I know. But so many people say to me, "But how can we?" As the tax collector does, it is clear: humbly, before God [Luke 18:9-14]. Each one, with humility, allowing themselves to be gazed upon by the Lord and imploring his goodness, that he may visit us.

But in the family, how is this done? After all, prayer seems to be something personal, and besides there is never a good time, a moment of peace. . . . Yes, all that is true enough, but it is also a matter of humility, of realizing that we need God, like the tax collector! And all families, we need God—all of us! We need his help, his strength, his blessing, his mercy, his forgiveness. And we need simplicity to pray as a family: simplicity is necessary! Praying the Our Father together, around the table, is not something extraordinary—it's easy. And praying the Rosary together, as a family, is very beautiful and a source of great strength! And also praying for one another! The husband for his wife, the wife for her husband, both together for their children, the children for their grandparents . . . praying for each other. This is what it means to pray in the family, and it is what makes the family strong: prayer.

—HOMILY FOR FAMILY DAY,
ST. PETER'S SQUARE, OCTOBER 27, 2013

Communicating with God

In the family we realize that others have preceded us; they made it possible for us to exist and, in our turn, to generate life and to do something good and beautiful. We can give because we have received. This virtuous circle is at the heart of the family's ability to communicate among its members and with others. More generally, it is the model for all communication.

The experience of this relationship which "precedes" us enables the family to become the setting in which the most basic form of communication, which is prayer, is handed down. When parents put their newborn children to sleep, they frequently entrust them to God, asking that he watch over them. When the children are a little older, parents help them to recite some simple prayers, thinking with affection of other people, such as grandparents, relatives, the sick and suffering, and all those in need of God's help. It was in our families that the majority of us learned the religious dimension of communication, which in the case of Christianity is permeated with love, the love that God bestows upon us and which we then offer to others.

—MESSAGE FOR WORLD COMMUNICATIONS DAY,
JANUARY 23, 2015

Jesus Says, "Come to Me"

What is most burdensome in life . . . is a lack of love. It weighs upon us never to receive a smile, not to be welcomed. Certain silences are oppressive, even at times within families, between husbands and wives, between parents and children, among siblings. Without love, the burden becomes even heavier, intolerable. I think of elderly people living alone, and families who receive no help in caring for someone at home with special needs. "Come to me, all who labor and are heavy laden," Jesus says (Matthew 11:28).

Dear families, the Lord knows our struggles; he knows them. He knows the burdens we have in our lives. But the Lord also knows our great desire to find joy and rest! Do you remember? Jesus said, " . . . that your joy may be complete" (cf. John 15:11). Jesus wants our joy to be complete! He said this to the apostles, and today he says it to us. Here, then, is the first thing I would like to share with you this evening, and it is a saying of Jesus. "Come to me, families from around the world," Jesus says, "and I will give you rest, so that your joy may be complete." Take home this word of Jesus, carry it in your hearts, share it with the family. It invites us to come to Jesus so that he may give this joy to us and to everyone.

—ADDRESS TO THE PILGRIMAGE OF FAMILIES,
ST. PETER'S SQUARE, OCTOBER 26, 2013

Forgive One Another

This is important—to know how to forgive one another in families because we all make mistakes, all of us! Sometimes we do things which are not good and which harm others. It is important to have the courage to ask for forgiveness when we are at fault in the family. . . . We all make mistakes, and on occasion someone gets offended in the marriage, in the family, and sometimes, I say, plates are smashed, harsh words are spoken, but please listen to my advice: don't ever let the sun set without reconciling. Peace is made each day in the family: "Please forgive me," and then you start over.

—ADDRESS TO THE PILGRIMAGE OF FAMILIES,
ST. PETER'S SQUARE, OCTOBER 26, 2013

The Families of Children with Disabilities

When it comes to the challenges of communication, families who have children with one or more disabilities have much to teach us. A motor, sensory, or mental limitation can be a reason for closing in on ourselves, but it can also become, thanks to the love of parents, siblings, and friends, an incentive to openness, sharing, and ready communication with all. It can also help schools, parishes, and associations to become more welcoming and inclusive of everyone.

—MESSAGE FOR WORLD COMMUNICATIONS DAY,
JANUARY 23, 2015

If There Is No Love, There Is No Joy

The Evangelist Luke tells us that the Blessed Mother and St. Joseph, in keeping with the Law of Moses, took the baby Jesus to the Temple to offer him to the Lord, and that an elderly man and woman, Simeon and Anna, moved by the Holy Spirit, went to meet them and acknowledged Jesus as the Messiah (cf. Luke 2:22-38). Simeon took him in his arms and thanked God that he had finally "seen" salvation. Anna, despite her advanced age, found new vigor and began to speak to everyone about the baby.

It is a beautiful image: two young parents and two elderly people, brought together by Jesus. He is the one who brings together and unites generations! He is the inexhaustible font of that love which overcomes every occasion of self-absorption, solitude, and sadness. In your journey as a family, you share so many beautiful moments: meals, rest, housework, leisure, prayer, trips and pilgrimages, and times of mutual support. . . . Nevertheless, if there is no love, then there is no joy, and authentic love comes to us from Jesus. He offers us his word, which illuminates our path; he gives us the Bread of Life, which sustains us on our journey.

—LETTER TO FAMILIES, FEBRUARY 2, 2014

The Gift of Wisdom

Think of a mother at her home with the children; when one does something, the other thinks of something else, and the poor mother goes to and fro with the problems of her children. And when mothers get tired and scold the children, is that wisdom? Scolding children—I ask you—is this wisdom? What do you say: is it wisdom or not? No!

Instead, when the mother takes her child aside and gently reproves him, saying, "Don't do this, because . . . ," and explains with great patience, is this the wisdom of God? Yes! It is what the Holy Spirit gives us in life! Then, in marriage, for example, the two spouses— the husband and wife—argue, and then they don't look at each other, or if they do look at each other, they look at each other with displeasure: is this the wisdom of God? No! Instead, if one says, "Ah well, the storm has passed, let's make peace," and they begin again and go forward in peace: is this wisdom? . . . Now, this is the gift of wisdom. May it come to our homes; may we have it with the children; may it come to us all!

—GENERAL AUDIENCE,
ST. PETER'S SQUARE, APRIL 9, 2014

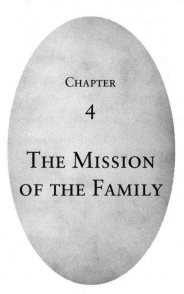

CHAPTER

4

THE MISSION
OF THE FAMILY

A Better Future for the World

The family is a community which provides help, which celebrates life and is fruitful. Once we realize this, we will once more be able to see how the family continues to be a rich human resource, as opposed to a problem or an institution in crisis. At times the media can tend to present the family as a kind of abstract model which has to be accepted or rejected, defended or attacked, rather than as a living reality. Or else a ground for ideological clashes rather than as a setting where we can all learn what it means to communicate in a love received and returned. Relating our experiences means realizing that our lives are bound together as a single reality, that our voices are many, and that each is unique.

Families should be seen as a resource rather than as a problem for society. Families at their best actively communicate by their witness the beauty and the richness of the relationship between man and woman, and between parents and children. We are not fighting to defend the past. Rather, with patience and trust, we are working to build a better future for the world in which we live.

—MESSAGE FOR WORLD COMMUNICATIONS DAY,
JANUARY 23, 2015

Prophetic Voices

The Gospel we have heard [Matthew 1:18-25] reminds us of our Christian duty to be *prophetic voices* in the midst of our communities. Joseph listened to the angel of the Lord and responded to God's call to care for Jesus and Mary. In this way he played his part in God's plan, and became a blessing not only for the Holy Family, but a blessing for all of humanity. With Mary, Joseph served as a model for the boy Jesus as he grew in wisdom, age, and grace (cf. Luke 2:52). When families bring children into the world, train them in faith and sound values, and teach them to contribute to society, they become a blessing in our world. Families can become a blessing for all of humanity! God's love becomes present and active by the way we love and by the good works that we do. We extend Christ's kingdom in this world. And in doing this, we prove faithful to the prophetic mission which we have received in Baptism.

—MEETING WITH FAMILIES, MALL OF ASIA ARENA, MANILA, JANUARY 16, 2015

The Fundamental Pillar

It is necessary to insist on the fundamental pillars that govern a nation: its intangible assets. The family is the foundation of coexistence and a guarantee against social fragmentation. Children have a right to grow up in a family with a father and a mother capable of creating a suitable environment for the child's growth and emotional development.

—HUMANUM COLLOQUIUM, ROME,
NOVEMBER 17, 2014

A New Mission Field

The Christian family, in fact, is the first community called to announce the Gospel to the human person during growth and to bring him or her, through a progressive education and catechesis, to full human and Christian maturity" (*Familiaris Consortio*, 2). Marital fidelity is above all the foundation upon which a harmonious family life can be built. Unfortunately, in our time we see that the family and marriage are undergoing a deep inner crisis in the countries of the Western world. . . . Globalization and postmodern individualism promote a lifestyle that makes it much more difficult to develop stable bonds between people, and it is not conducive to promoting a culture of the family.

This opens up a new mission field for the Church; for example, among groups of families where opportunities are created for interpersonal relationships and for a relationship with God, where authentic communion that welcomes everyone equally can grow, that does not close itself off into groups of the elite, that heals wounds, builds bridges, goes in search of the lost, and helps "to bear one another's burdens" (Galatians 6:2).

—ADDRESS TO THE BISHOPS OF AUSTRIA,
JANUARY 30, 2014

Sharing the Story of Life

It is significant how—even in the individualistic culture which distorts bonds and renders them ephemeral—in each person born of woman, there remains alive an essential need for stability, for an open door, for someone with whom to weave and to share the story of life, a history to belong to. The communion of life embraced by spouses, their openness to the gift of life, the mutual protection, the encounter and the memory of generations, educational support, the transmission of the Christian faith to their children … with all this the family continues to be a school unparalleled in humanity, an indispensable contribution to a just and supportive society (cf. *Evangelii Gaudium,* 66–68). And the deeper its roots, the more possible it is in life to go out and go far, without getting lost or feeling a stranger in a foreign land.

—ADDRESS DURING THE MEETING ON THE FAMILY,
ST. PETER'S SQUARE, OCTOBER 4, 2014

Value the Family

The family stands at the center of society's hopes and struggles. With renewed conviction, the Church continues to encourage the commitment of all, individuals and institutions, in order to support the family, which is the primary place where the human being is formed and grows and where upright values and examples are learned. The family needs stability and the recognition of its mutual bonds in order to carry out its irreplaceable task and to fulfill its mission. It needs to be appreciated, valued, and protected as it puts its energy at the service of society.

—Address to the President of Italy, Quirinal Palace, November 14, 2013

Dangers to the Family

The gift of the Holy Family was entrusted to St. Joseph so that he could care for it. Each of you, each of us—for I, too, am part of a family—is charged with caring for God's plan. The angel of the Lord revealed to Joseph the dangers which threatened Jesus and Mary, forcing them to flee to Egypt and then to settle in Nazareth. So too, in our time, God calls upon us to recognize the dangers threatening our own families and to protect them from harm.

Let us be on guard against colonization by new ideologies. There are forms of ideological colonization which are out to destroy the family. They are not born of dreams, of prayers, of closeness to God or the mission which God gave us; they come from without, and for that reason I am saying that they are forms of colonization. Let's not lose the freedom of the mission which God has given us, the mission of the family. Just as our peoples, at a certain moment of their history, were mature enough to say "no" to all forms of political colonization, so too in our families we need to be very wise, very shrewd, very strong in order to say "no" to all attempts at an ideological colonization of our families. We need to ask St. Joseph, the friend of the angel, to send us the inspiration to know when we can say "yes" and when we have to say "no."

—MEETING WITH FAMILIES, MALL OF ASIA ARENA,
MANILA, JANUARY 16, 2015

Fostering a New Human Ecology

Marriage and the family are in crisis today. We now live in a culture of the temporary, in which more and more people reject marriage as a public obligation. This revolution of customs and morals has often waved "the flag of freedom," but it has, in reality, brought spiritual and material devastation to countless human beings, especially the poorest and most vulnerable. It is ever more evident that the decline of the culture of marriage is associated with increased poverty and a host of other social ills that disproportionately affect women, children, and the elderly. It is always they who suffer the most in this crisis.

The crisis of the family has produced a human ecological crisis, for social environments, like natural environments, need protection. Although humanity has come to understand the need to address the conditions that threaten our natural environment, we have been slow—we have been slow in our culture, even in our Catholic culture—we have been slow to recognize

that even our social environments are at risk. It is therefore essential that we foster a new human ecology and
make it move forward.

—HUMANUM COLLOQUIUM, ROME,
NOVEMBER 17, 2014

Family Is Family!

We must not fall into the trap of being limited by ideological concepts. The family is an anthropological fact, and consequently a social, cultural fact. We cannot qualify it with ideological concepts which are compelling at only one moment in history and then decline. Today there can be no talk of the *conservative family* or the *progressive family*: family is family! Do not allow yourselves to be qualified by this, or by other ideological concepts. The family has a force of its own.

—HUMANUM COLLOQUIUM, ROME,
NOVEMBER 17, 2014

A Lifelong Covenant of Love

The holiness and indissolubility of Christian matrimony, often disintegrating under tremendous pressure from the secular world, must be deepened by clear doctrine and supported by the witness of committed married couples. Christian matrimony is a lifelong covenant of love between one man and one woman; it entails real sacrifices in order to turn away from illusory notions of sexual freedom and in order to foster conjugal fidelity.

—ADDRESS TO THE BISHOPS OF SOUTH AFRICA,
APRIL 25, 2014

Protect Your Families!

Our world needs . . . holy and loving families to protect the beauty and truth of the family in God's plan and to be a support and example for other families. Every threat to the family is a threat to society itself. The future of humanity, as St. John Paul II often said, passes through the family (cf. *Familiaris Consortio*, 85). The future passes through the family. So protect your families! Protect your families! See in them your country's greatest treasure and nourish them always by prayer and the grace of the sacraments.

Families will always have their trials, but may you never add to them! Instead, be living examples of love, forgiveness, and care. Be sanctuaries of respect for life, proclaiming the sacredness of every human life from conception to natural death. What a gift this would be to society, if every Christian family lived fully its noble vocation! So rise with Jesus and Mary, and set out on the path the Lord traces for each of you.

—MEETING WITH FAMILIES, MALL OF ASIA ARENA,
MANILA, JANUARY 16, 2015

A Cultural Crisis

The family is experiencing a profound cultural crisis, as are all communities and social bonds. In the case of the family, the weakening of these bonds is particularly serious because the family is the fundamental cell of society, where we learn to live with others despite our differences and to belong to one another; it is also the place where parents pass on the faith to their children. Marriage now tends to be viewed as a form of mere emotional satisfaction that can be constructed in any way or modified at will. But the indispensable contribution of marriage to society transcends the feelings and momentary needs of the couple. As the French bishops have taught, it is not born "of loving sentiment, ephemeral by definition, but from the depth of the obligation assumed by the spouses who accept to enter a total communion of life."

— Apostolic exhortation *Evangelii Gaudium*, 66

Make Known God's Plan for the Family

Today the family is looked down upon and mistreated. We are called to acknowledge how beautiful, true, and good it is to start a family, to be a family today, and how indispensable the family is for the life of the world and for the future of humanity. We are called to make known God's magnificent plan for the family and to help spouses joyfully experience this plan in their lives, as we accompany them amidst so many difficulties with a pastoral care that is sound, courageous, and full of love.

—ADDRESS AT THE EXTRAORDINARY CONSISTORY ON THE FAMILY, NEW SYNOD HALL, FEBRUARY 20, 2014

The Foundation of Humanity

Not only would I say that the family is important for the evangelization of the . . . world. The family is important, and it is necessary for the survival of humanity. Without the family, the cultural survival of the human race would be at risk. The family, whether we like it or not, is the foundation.

—INTERVIEW, RIO DE JANEIRO, JULY 27, 2013

Bricks for the Building Up of Society

It is impossible to quantify the strength and depth of humanity contained in a family: mutual help, educational support, relationships developing as family members mature, the sharing of joys and difficulties. Families are the first place in which we are formed as persons and, at the same time, the "bricks" for the building up of society.

—HOMILY AT MASS FOR THE RITE OF MARRIAGE,
ST. PETER'S SQUARE, SEPTEMBER 14, 2014

Remain Steadfast

The individualism of our postmodern and globalized era favors a lifestyle which weakens the development and stability of personal relationships and distorts family bonds. Pastoral activity needs to bring out more clearly the fact that our relationship with the Father demands and encourages a communion which heals, promotes, and reinforces interpersonal bonds. In our world, especially in some countries, different forms of war and conflict are reemerging, yet we Christians remain steadfast in our intention to respect others, to heal wounds, to build bridges, to strengthen relationships, and to "bear one another's burdens" (Galatians 6:2).

—APOSTOLIC EXHORTATION *EVANGELII GAUDIUM*, 67

Children Are a Sign

Today . . . children are a sign. They are a sign of hope, a sign of life, but also a "diagnostic" sign, a marker indicating the health of families, society, and the entire world. Wherever children are accepted, loved, cared for, and protected, the family is healthy, society is more healthy, and the world is more human.

—HOMILY, MANGER SQUARE, BETHLEHEM, MAY 25, 2014

Take Care of One Another

The family . . . is the teacher of acceptance and solidarity: it is within the family that education substantially draws upon relationships of solidarity; in the family one learns that the loss of health is not a reason for discriminating against human life; the family teaches us not to fall into individualism and to balance the "I" with the "we."

It is there that "taking care of one another" becomes a foundation of human life and a moral attitude to foster, through the values of commitment and solidarity. The witness of the family is crucial, before the whole of society, in reaffirming the importance of an elderly person as a member of a community, who has his or her own mission to accomplish and who only seemingly receives with nothing to offer.

—MESSAGE TO THE PONTIFICAL ACADEMY OF LIFE,
FEBRUARY 19, 2014

A Beautiful and Brave Testimony

We cannot ignore the hardship of many families that is due to unemployment, the problem of housing, the practical impossibility of freely choosing their own educational curriculum; the suffering that is also due to internal conflicts within families, to the failures of the conjugal and family experience and to the violence that unfortunately lurks in families and wreaks havoc even in our homes. We owe it to all and wish to be particularly close to them with respect and with a true sense of brotherhood and solidarity. However, we want above all to remember the simple but beautiful and brave testimony of so many families who joyfully live the experience of marriage and parenthood enlightened and sustained by the Lord's grace and fearlessly face even moments of the cross. Lived in union with the cross of the Lord, the cross does not hinder the path of love but, on the contrary, can make it stronger and fuller.

—MESSAGE TO ITALIAN CATHOLICS, SEPTEMBER 11, 2013

The Privileged School for Learning

The family is the privileged school for learning generosity, sharing, responsibility, a school that teaches how to overcome a certain individualistic mind-set which has worked its way into our societies. Sustaining and promoting families, making the most of their fundamental and central role, means working for a just and supportive development.

—MESSAGE TO ITALIAN CATHOLICS, SEPTEMBER 11, 2013

The Courage to Defend Openness to Life

I think of Blessed Paul VI. At a time when the problem of population growth was being raised, he had the courage to defend openness to life in families. He knew the difficulties that are there in every family, and so in his encyclical [*Humanae Vitae*], he was very merciful towards particular cases, and he asked confessors to be very merciful and understanding in dealing with particular cases. But he also had a broader vision: he looked at the peoples of the earth and he saw this threat of families being destroyed for lack of children. Paul VI was courageous; he was a good pastor, and he warned his flock of the wolves who were coming. From his place in heaven, may he bless this evening!

—MEETING WITH FAMILIES, MALL OF ASIA ARENA, MANILA, JANUARY 16, 2015

Leaven in the Dough

For the Christian community, the family is far more than a "theme": it is life, it is the daily fabric of life; it is the journey of generations who pass on the faith together with love and with the basic moral values. It is concrete solidarity, effort, patience, and also a project, hope, a future. All this, which the Christian community lives out in the light of faith, hope, and charity, should never be kept to oneself but must become, every day, the leaven in the dough of the whole of society for its greater common good.

—MESSAGE TO ITALIAN CATHOLICS, SEPTEMBER 11, 2013

TO CHILDREN AND YOUNG PEOPLE

Jesus Gives Us Strength

This is the Christian life: talking to the Father, talking to the Son, and talking to the Holy Spirit. Jesus has saved us, but he also walks beside us in life. Is this true? And how does he walk? What does he do when he walks beside us in life? This is hard. Anyone who knows this wins the Derby! What does Jesus do when he walks with us? . . . First: he helps us. He leads us! Very good. He walks with us, he helps us, he leads us, and he teaches us to journey on.

And Jesus also gives us the strength to work. Doesn't he? He sustains us! Good! In difficulty, doesn't he? And also in our school tasks! He supports us, he helps us, he leads us, he sustains us. That's it! Jesus always goes with us. Good. But listen, Jesus gives us strength. How does Jesus give us strength? You know this, you know that he gives us strength! . . . In Communion he gives us strength, he really helps us with strength. He comes to us. But when you say, "He gives us Communion," does a piece of bread make you so strong? Isn't it bread? Is it bread? This is bread, but is what is on the altar bread? Or isn't it bread? It seems to be bread. It is not really bread. What is it? It is the Body of Jesus. Jesus comes into our hearts.

—Homily to First Communicants,
May 26, 2013

Put on Faith

Put on faith": what does this mean? When we prepare a plate of food and we see that it needs salt, well, we "put on" salt; when it needs oil, then you "put on" oil. "To put on," that is, to place on top of, to pour over. And so it is in our life, dear young friends: if we want it to have real meaning and fulfillment, as you want and as you deserve, I say to each one of you, "Put on faith," and life will take on a new flavor, life will have a compass to show you the way. "Put on hope," and every one of your days will be enlightened and your horizon will no longer be dark but luminous. "Put on love," and your life will be like a house built on rock; your journey will be joyful because you will find many friends to journey with you. Put on faith, put on hope, put on love! . . .

But who can give us all this? In the Gospel we hear the answer: Christ. "This is my Son, my chosen one. Listen to him!" Jesus brings God to us and us to God. With him our life is transformed and renewed, and we can see reality with new eyes, from Jesus' standpoint, with his own eyes (cf. *Lumen Fidei,* 18). For this reason, I say to every one of you today: "Put on Christ!" in your life, and you will find a friend in whom you can always trust; "Put on Christ," and you will see the wings of hope spreading and letting you journey with joy towards the future; "Put on Christ," and your life will be full of his love; it will be a fruitful life. Because we all want to have a fruitful life, one that is life-giving for others.

—Welcoming Ceremony at Waterfront,
World Youth Day, Rio de Janiero, July 25, 2013

Let Yourselves Be Loved by Christ

Dear young people: "Put on Christ" in your lives. In these days, Christ awaits you in his word; listen carefully to him and his presence will arouse your heart. "Put on Christ": he awaits you in the Sacrament of Penance; with his mercy he will cure all the wounds caused by sin. Do not be afraid to ask God's forgiveness, because he never tires of forgiving us, like a father who loves us. God is pure mercy! "Put on Christ": he is waiting for you also in the Eucharist, the sacrament of his presence and his sacrifice of love, and he is waiting for you also in the humanity of the many young people who will enrich you with their friendship, encourage you by their witness to the faith, and teach you the language of love, goodness, and service.

You too, dear young people, can be joyful witnesses of his love, courageous witnesses of his Gospel, carrying to this world a ray of his light. Let yourselves be loved by Christ; he is a friend that will not disappoint.

—Welcoming Ceremony at Waterfront,
World Youth Day, Rio de Janiero, July 25, 2013

You are Unique but Not Alone!

You, boys and girls, . . . each one of you is the unique fruit of love, you come from love and you grow in love. You are *unique but not alone!* And the fact of having brothers and sisters is good for you: the sons and daughters of a large family are more capable of fraternal communion even from early childhood. In a world often marked by selfishness, a large family is a school of solidarity and sharing; and this attitude is to the benefit of society as a whole.

—ADDRESS TO THE ITALIAN ASSOCIATION OF LARGE FAMILIES,
DECEMBER 28, 2014

Be Builders of the World

Your young hearts want to build a better world. I have been closely following the news reports of the many young people who throughout the world have taken to the streets in order to express their desire for a more just and fraternal society. Young people in the streets. It is the young who want to be the protagonists of change. Please, don't leave it to others to be the protagonists of change. You are the ones who hold the future! . . . Through you, the future is fulfilled in the world. I ask you also to be protagonists of this transformation. Continue to overcome apathy, offering a Christian response to the social and political anxieties which are arising in various parts of the world. I ask you to be builders of the world, to work for a better world. Dear young people, please, don't be observers of life but get involved. Jesus did not remain an observer, but he immersed himself. Don't be observers but immerse yourself in the reality of life, as Jesus did.

But one question remains: Where do we start? Whom do we ask to begin this work? Some people once asked Mother Teresa of Calcutta what needed to change in the Church, and which wall should they start with? They asked her, "Where is the starting point?" And she replied, "You and I are the starting point!" This woman showed determination! She knew where to start. And today I make her words my own and I say to you: shall we begin? Where? With you and me! Each one of you, once again in silence, ask yourself: if I must begin with myself, where exactly do I start? Each one of you, open his or her heart, so that Jesus may tell you where to start.

—Prayer Vigil with Young People, World Youth Day, Rio de Janiero, July 27, 2013

God Shows Up with Surprises

True love is both loving and letting oneself be loved. It is harder to let ourselves be loved than it is to love. That is why it is so hard to achieve the perfect love of God, because we can love him, but the important thing is to let ourselves be loved by him. True love is being open to that love which was there first and catches us by surprise. If all you have is information, you are closed to surprises. Love makes you open to surprises. Love is always a surprise because it starts with a dialogue between two persons: the one who loves and the one who is loved. We say that God is the God of surprises because he always loved us first, and he waits to take us by surprise. God surprises us. Let's allow ourselves to be surprised by God. Let's not have the psychology of a computer, thinking that we know everything. What do I mean? Think for a moment: the computer has all the answers: never a surprise. In the challenge of love, God shows up with surprises. . . .

So let yourselves be surprised by God! Don't be afraid of surprises, afraid that they will shake you up.

They make us insecure, but they change the direction we are going in. True love makes you "burn life," even at the risk of coming up empty-handed. Think of St. Francis: he left everything; he died with empty hands but with a full heart.

—Meeting with Young People,
St. Thomas University, Manila, January 18, 2015

The Lord Needs You!

I think of the story of St. Francis of Assisi. In front of the crucifix, he heard the voice of Jesus saying to him, "Francis, go, rebuild my house." The young Francis responded readily and generously to the Lord's call to rebuild his house. But which house? Slowly but surely, Francis came to realize that it was not a question of repairing a stone building but about doing his part for the life of the Church. It was a matter of being at the service of the Church, loving her and working to make the countenance of Christ shine ever more brightly in her.

Today too, as always, the Lord needs you, young people, for his Church. My friends, the Lord needs you! Today too he is calling each of you to follow him in his Church and to be missionaries. The Lord is calling you today! Not the masses, but you, and you, and you, each one of you. Listen to what he is saying to you in your heart.

—PRAYER VIGIL WITH YOUNG PEOPLE, WORLD YOUTH DAY, RIO DE JANIERO, JULY 27, 2013

"Go," "Do Not Be Afraid," and "Serve"

Three ideas: "Go," "Do not be afraid," and "Serve." . . . If you follow these three ideas, you will experience that the one who evangelizes is evangelized; the one who transmits the joy of faith receives more joy. Dear young friends, . . . do not be afraid to be generous with Christ, to bear witness to his Gospel. . . . When God sends the prophet Jeremiah, he gives him the power to "pluck up and to break down, to destroy and to overthrow, to build and to plant" (1:10). It is the same for you. Bringing the Gospel is bringing God's power to pluck up and break down evil and violence, to destroy and overthrow the barriers of selfishness, intolerance, and hatred so as to build a new world.

Dear young friends, Jesus Christ is counting on you! The Church is counting on you! The Pope is counting on you! May Mary, Mother of Jesus and our Mother, always accompany you with her tenderness: "Go and make disciples of all nations." Amen.

—Homily, World Youth Day, Rio de Janiero, July 28, 2013

Swim against the Tide

God calls you to make definitive choices, and he has a plan for each of you: to discover that plan and to respond to your vocation is to move toward personal fulfillment. God calls each of us to be holy, to live his life, but he has a particular path for each one of us. Some are called to holiness through family life in the Sacrament of Marriage. Today there are those who say that marriage is out of fashion. Is it out of fashion? In a culture of relativism and the ephemeral, many preach the importance of "enjoying" the moment. They say that it is not worth making a lifelong commitment, making a definitive decision, "forever," because we do not know what tomorrow will bring. I ask you, instead, to be revolutionaries; I ask you to swim against the tide; yes, I am asking you to rebel against this culture that sees everything as temporary and that ultimately believes you are incapable of responsibility, that believes you are incapable of true love. I have confidence in you and I pray for you.

—MEETING WITH THE VOLUNTEERS OF WORLD YOUTH DAY,
RIO DE JANEIRO, JULY 28, 2013

The Challenge to Love

You can ask me: "Father, how can I become wise?" This is another challenge: the challenge of love. What is the most important lesson which you have to learn at the university? What is the most important lesson that you have to learn in life? It is learning how to love. This is the challenge which life sets before you today. Learning how to love. Not just how to accumulate information. There comes a time when you don't know what to do with it all. It's a storehouse. Unless, through love, all this information can bear fruit.

For this to happen, the Gospel proposes to us a serene and tranquil thing to do. It is to use the three languages: the language of the mind, the language of the heart, and the language of the hands. All three together, harmoniously: what you think, you feel, and you do. Your information descends to the heart, moves it, and gets translated into action. And all this in a harmonious way: I think what I feel and do, I feel what I think and what I do, and I do what I think and what I feel.

—Meeting with Young People ,
St. Thomas University, Manila, January 18, 2015

127

It Is Worth Saying Yes to God

The Lord calls some to be priests, to give themselves to him more fully so as to love all people with the heart of the Good Shepherd. Some he calls to the service of others in the religious life: devoting themselves in monasteries to praying for the good of the world and in various areas of the apostolate, giving of themselves for the sake of all, especially those most in need. I will never forget that day, September 21—I was seventeen years old—when, after stopping in the Church of San José de Flores to go to Confession, I first heard God calling me. Do not be afraid of what God asks of you! It is worth saying "yes" to God. In him we find joy!

Dear young people, some of you may not yet know what you will do with your lives. Ask the Lord, and he will show you the way. The young Samuel kept hearing the voice of the Lord who was calling him, but he did not understand or know what to say, yet with the help of the priest Eli, in the end he answered, "Speak, Lord, for I am listening" (cf. 1 Samuel 3:1-10). You too can ask the Lord, "What do you want me to do? What path am I to follow?"

—Meeting with the Volunteers of World Youth Day, Rio de Janeiro, July 28, 2013

Rediscover the Vocation to Love

Youth is a time of life when your desire for a love which is genuine, beautiful, and expansive begins to blossom in your hearts. How powerful is this ability to love and to be loved! Do not let this precious treasure be debased, destroyed, or spoiled. That is what happens when we start to use our neighbors for our own selfish ends, even as objects of pleasure. Hearts are broken and sadness follows upon these negative experiences. I urge you: do not be afraid of true love, the love that Jesus teaches us and which St. Paul describes as "patient and kind" (cf. 1 Corinthians 13:4-8). . . .

In encouraging you to rediscover the beauty of the human vocation to love, I also urge you to rebel against the widespread tendency to reduce love to something banal, reducing it to its sexual aspect alone, deprived of its essential characteristics of beauty, communion, fidelity, and responsibility. . . .

You young people are brave adventurers! If you allow yourselves to discover the rich teachings of the Church on love, you will discover that Christianity does not consist of a series of prohibitions which stifle our desire for happiness, but rather a project for life capable of captivating our hearts.

—Message for the 30th World Youth Day,
January 31, 2015

Are You Praying?

My question to you is this: "Are you praying?" Do you know that you can speak with Jesus, with the Father, with the Holy Spirit as you speak to a friend? And not just any friend, but the greatest and most trusted of your friends! . . .

Once again I invite you to encounter the Lord by frequently reading sacred Scripture. If you are not already in the habit of doing so, begin with the Gospels. Read a line or two each day. Let God's word speak to your heart and enlighten your path (cf. Psalm 119:105). You will discover that God can be "seen" also in the faces of your brothers and sisters, especially those who are most forgotten: the poor, the hungry, those who thirst, strangers, the sick, those imprisoned (cf. Matthew 25:31-46). Have you ever had this experience? Dear young people, in order to enter into the logic of the kingdom of heaven, we must recognize that we are poor with the poor. A pure heart is necessarily one which has been stripped bare, a heart that knows how to bend down and share its life with those most in need.

Encountering God in prayer, the reading of the Bible, and in the fraternal life will help you better to know the Lord and yourselves. Like the disciples on the way to Emmaus (cf. Luke 24:13-35), the Lord's voice will make your hearts burn within you. He will open your eyes to recognize his presence and to discover the loving plan he has for your life.

—Message for the 30th World Youth Day,
January 31, 2015

Honor Your Father and Your Mother

The fourth commandment asks children—we are all children!—to honor our father and mother (cf. Exodus 20:12). This commandment comes immediately after those regarding God himself. Indeed, it contains something sacred, something divine, something which lies at the root of every other type of respect among men. And to the biblical formulation of the fourth commandment is added: "that your days may be long in the land which the Lord your God gives you." The virtuous bond between generations is the guarantee of the future, and is the guarantee of a truly human history. A society with children who do not honor parents is a society without honor; when one does not honor one's parents, one loses one's own honor!

—GENERAL AUDIENCE,
ST. PETER'S SQUARE, FEBRUARY 11, 2015

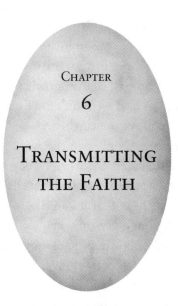

CHAPTER

6

TRANSMITTING
THE FAITH

The Window of the Young

Here it is common for parents to say, "Our children are the apple of our eyes." What a beautiful expression of Brazilian wisdom this is, applying to young people an image drawn from our eyes, which are the window through which light enters into us, granting us the miracle of sight! What would become of us if we didn't look after our eyes? How could we move forward? . . .

Listen! Young people are the window through which the future enters the world. They are the window, and so they present us with great challenges. Our generation will show that it can rise to the promise found in each young person when we know how to give them space. This means that we have to create the material and spiritual conditions for their full development; to give them a solid basis on which to build their lives; to guarantee their safety and their education to be everything they can be; to pass on to them lasting values that make life worth living; to give them a transcendent horizon for their thirst for authentic happiness and their creativity for the good; to give them the legacy of a world worthy of human life; and to awaken in them their greatest potential as builders of their own destiny, sharing responsibility for the future of everyone. If we can do all this, we anticipate today the future that enters the world through the window of the young.

—WELCOMING CEREMONY AT PALACE,
WORLD YOUTH DAY, RIO DE JANIERO, JULY 22, 2013

A Link in the Chain

In effect, as from generation to generation life is transmitted, so too from generation to generation, through rebirth at the baptismal font, grace is transmitted, and by this grace the Christian people journeys through time, like a river that irrigates the land and spreads God's blessing throughout the world. From the moment that Jesus said what we heard in the Gospel reading [Mark 1:29-39], the disciples went out to baptize; and from that time until today, there is a chain in the transmission of the faith through Baptism. And each one of us is a link in that chain: a step forward, always, like a river that irrigates. Such is the grace of God and such is our faith, which we must transmit to our sons and daughters, transmit to children, so that once adults, they can do the same for their children.

—GENERAL AUDIENCE,
ST. PETER'S SQUARE, JANUARY 15, 2014

Mothers Plant the Seed of Faith

A society without mothers would be a dehumanized society, for mothers are always, even in the worst moments, witnesses of tenderness, dedication, and moral strength. Mothers often pass on the deepest sense of religious practice: in a human being's life, the value of faith is inscribed in the first prayers, the first acts of devotion that a child learns. It is a message that believing mothers are able to pass on without much explanation: these come later, but the seed of faith is those early precious moments. Without mothers, not only would there be no new faithful, but the faith would lose a good part of its simple and profound warmth.

—GENERAL AUDIENCE,
PAUL VI HALL, JANUARY 7, 2015

From Whom Did We Receive Our Faith?

No one becomes Christian on his or her own. If we believe, if we know how to pray, if we acknowledge the Lord and can listen to his word, if we feel him close to us and recognize him in our brothers and sisters, it is because others, before us, lived the faith and then transmitted it to us. We have received the faith from our fathers, from our ancestors, and they have instructed us in it. If we think about it carefully, who knows how many beloved faces pass before our eyes at this moment: it could be the face of our parents who requested our Baptism; that of our grandparents or of some family member who taught us how to make the Sign of the Cross and to recite our first prayers.

—General Audience, St. Peter's Square, June 25, 2014

The Home Where Mary Grew Up

The Church celebrates the parents of the Virgin Mary, the grandparents of Jesus, Saints Joachim and Anne. In their home Mary came into the world, accompanied by the extraordinary mystery of the Immaculate Conception. Mary grew up in the home of Joachim and Anne; she was surrounded by their love and faith; in their home she learned to listen to the Lord and to follow his will. Saints Joachim and Anne were part of a long chain of people who had transmitted their faith and love for God, expressed in the warmth and love of family life, down to Mary, who received the Son of God in her womb and who gave him to the world, to us. How precious is the family as the privileged place for transmitting the faith!

—ANGELUS, RIO DE JANIERO, JULY 26, 2013

My First Christian Proclamation

I had the great blessing of growing up in a family in which faith was lived in a simple, practical way. However, it was my paternal grandmother, in particular, who influenced my journey of faith. She was a woman who explained to us, who talked to us about Jesus, who taught us the catechism. I always remember that on the evening of Good Friday, she would take us to the candlelight procession, and at the end of this procession, "the dead Christ" would arrive, and our grandmother would make us—the children—kneel down, and she would say to us, "Look, he is dead, but tomorrow he will rise."

This was how I received my first Christian proclamation, from this very woman, from my grandmother! This is really beautiful! The first proclamation at home, in the family! And this makes me think of the love of so many mothers and grandmothers in the transmission of faith. They are the ones who pass on the faith. This used to happen in the early Church too, for St. Paul said to Timothy, "I am reminded of the faith of your mother and of your grandmother" (cf. 2 Timothy 1:5).

All the mothers and all the grandmothers who are here should think about this: passing on the faith! Because God sets beside us people who help us on our journey of faith. We do not find our faith in the abstract, no! It is always a person preaching who tells us who Jesus is, who communicates faith to us and gives us the first proclamation. And this is how I received my first experience of faith.

—ADDRESS TO ECCLESIAL MOVEMENTS,
ST. PETER'S SQUARE, MAY 18, 2013

The Importance of Confirmation

It is important to take care that our children, our young people, receive this sacrament [of Confirmation]. We all take care that they are baptized, and this is good, but perhaps we do not take so much care to ensure that they are confirmed. Thus, they remain at a midpoint in their journey and do not receive the Holy Spirit, who is so important in the Christian life since he gives us the strength to go on.

Let us think a little, each one of us: do we truly care whether our children, our young people, receive Confirmation? This is important; it is important! And if you have children or adolescents at home who have not yet received it and are at the age to do so, do everything possible to ensure that they complete their Christian initiation and receive the power of the Holy Spirit. It is important!

—GENERAL AUDIENCE,
ST. PETER'S SQUARE, JANUARY 29, 2014

Saving the Faith

Grandparents, who have received the blessing to see their children's children (cf. Psalm 128:6), are entrusted with a great responsibility: to transmit their life experience, their family history, the history of a community, of a people; to share wisdom with simplicity, and the faith itself—the most precious heritage! Happy is the family who have grandparents close by! A grandfather is a father twice over and a grandmother is a mother twice over. In those countries where religious persecution has been cruel—I am thinking, for instance, of Albania, where I was last Sunday—in those countries it was the grandparents who brought the children to be baptized in secret, to give them the faith. Well done! They were brave in persecution, and they saved the faith in those countries!

ADDRESS AT A MEETING WITH THE ELDERLY,
ST. PETER'S SQUARE, SEPTEMBER 28, 2014

Let Us Be Lights of Hope!

It is true that nowadays, to some extent, everyone, including our young people, feels attracted by the many idols which take the place of God and appear to offer hope: money, success, power, pleasure. Often a growing sense of loneliness and emptiness in the hearts of many people leads them to seek satisfaction in these ephemeral idols. Dear brothers and sisters, let us be lights of hope! Let us maintain a positive outlook on reality. Let us encourage the generosity which is typical of the young and help them to work actively in building a better world. Young people are a powerful engine for the Church and for society. They do not need material things alone; also and above all, they need to have held up to them those nonmaterial values which are the spiritual heart of a people, the memory of a people. In this Shrine, which is part of the memory of Brazil, we can almost read those values: spirituality, generosity, solidarity, perseverance, fraternity, joy; they are values whose deepest root is in the Christian faith.

—HOMILY, OUR LADY OF THE CONCEPTION OF APARECIDA,
BRAZIL, JULY 24, 2013

Evangelization Begins in the Home

The work of evangelization begins in the home. . . . Moreover, the Church's love for and pastoral solicitude towards the family is at the heart of the new evangelization. By promoting prayer, marital fidelity, monogamy, purity, and humble service of one another within families, the Church continues to make an invaluable contribution . . . , one which, coupled with her educational and healthcare apostolates, will surely foster greater stability and progress in your country. There is scarcely a finer service which the Church can offer than to give witness to our conviction of the sanctity of God's gift of life and to the essential role played by spiritual and stable families in preparing the younger generations to live virtuous lives and to face the challenges of the future with wisdom, courage, and generosity.

—ADDRESS TO THE BISHOPS OF TANZANIA, APRIL 7, 2014

CHAPTER

7

GRANDPARENTS AND THE ELDERLY

Memory and Promise

The memory of our elderly people sustains us as we journey on. The future of society, and precisely of Italian society, is rooted in the elderly and in the young: the latter, because they have the strength and are of the age to carry history ahead; the former, because they are a living memory. A people that does not take care of its elderly, its children, and its youth has no future, because it abuses both memory and promise.

—MESSAGE TO ITALIAN CATHOLICS, SEPTEMBER 11, 2013

Children Learn from Their Grandparents

Let me ask you: do you listen to your grandparents? Do you open your hearts to the memories that your grandparents pass on? Grandparents are like the wisdom of the family; they are the wisdom of a people. And a people that does not listen to grandparents is one that dies! Listen to your grandparents. Mary and Joseph are the family, sanctified by the presence of Jesus who is the fulfillment of all God's promises. Like the Holy Family of Nazareth, every family is part of the history of a people; it cannot exist without the generations who have gone before it. Therefore, today we have grandparents and children. The children learn from their grandparents, from the previous generation.

—ADDRESS TO THE PILGRIMAGE OF FAMILIES,
ST. PETER'S SQUARE, OCTOBER 26, 2013

Ecumenical Preaching from My Grandmother

When I was four years old—it was 1940, none of you were born yet!—I went out with my grandmother. In that time, it was thought that all Protestants went to hell. On the other side of the sidewalk there were two women of the Salvation Army. . . . And I remember like it was yesterday; I said to my grandmother, "Who are they? Nuns?" And my grandmother said, "No, they are Protestants, but they are good." Therefore, because of your good witness, my grandmother opened the door to ecumenism to me. The first ecumenical preaching I ever heard was in front of you.

—ADDRESS TO A DELEGATION OF THE SALVATION ARMY,
DECEMBER 12, 2014

Let Us Salute Grandparents

How important grandparents are for family life, for passing on the human and religious heritage which is so essential for each and every society! How important it is to have intergenerational exchanges and dialogue, especially within the context of the family. The *Aparecida* document says, "Children and the elderly build the future of peoples: children because they lead history forward, the elderly because they transmit the experience and wisdom of their lives" (447). This relationship and this dialogue between generations is a treasure to be preserved and strengthened! Grandparents: let us salute grandparents. Young people salute their grandparents with great affection, and they thank them for the ongoing witness of their wisdom.

—ANGELUS, RIO DE JANIERO, JULY 26, 2013

The Power of a Grandparent's Prayer

In a special way, old age is a time of grace, in which the Lord renews his call to us: he calls us to safeguard and transmit the faith, he calls us to pray, especially to intercede; he calls us to be close to those in need. . . . The elderly, grandparents, have the ability to understand the most difficult of situations: a great ability! And when they pray for these situations, their prayer is strong; it is powerful!

ADDRESS AT A MEETING WITH THE ELDERLY,
ST. PETER'S SQUARE, SEPTEMBER 28, 2014

"Sanctuaries" of Humanity

Not every older person, grandfather, grandmother has a family who can take him or her in. And so homes for the elderly are welcome. May they be real homes and not prisons! And may they be for the elderly, and not for the interests of anyone else! They must not be institutions where the elderly live forgotten, hidden, and neglected. I feel close to the many elderly who live in these institutions, and I think with gratitude of those who go to visit and care for them. Homes for the elderly should be the "lungs" of humanity in a town, a neighborhood, or a parish. They should be the "sanctuaries" of humanity where one who is old and weak is cared for and protected like a big brother or sister. It is so good to go visit an elderly person! Look at our children: sometimes we see them listless and sad; they go visit an elderly person and become joyful!

ADDRESS AT A MEETING WITH THE ELDERLY,
ST. PETER'S SQUARE, SEPTEMBER 28, 2014

May the Lord Give Us Wise Elders

Perhaps there are people missing here, perhaps the most important of all: grandparents! The elderly are not here, yet they are the "insurance" of our faith, the "old folks." When Mary and Joseph brought Jesus to the Temple (Luke 2:22-38), two of them were there, and, unless I am mistaken, four if not five times the Gospel says that "they were led by the Holy Spirit." But it says of Mary and Joseph that they were led by the law. Young people must carry out the law; the elderly—like good wine—have the freedom of the Holy Spirit. And so this Simeon, who was courageous, invented a "liturgy" and praised God; he was praising . . . and it was the Spirit who impelled him to do so.

The elderly! They are our wisdom, they are the wisdom of the Church—the elderly whom we so often discard, grandparents, the elderly . . . And that little old lady, Anna, did something extraordinary in the Church: she canonized gossip! How did she do it? Like this: instead of gossiping about somebody else, she went all over town talking about Jesus: "He is the one; he is the one who is going to save us!" (cf. 2:38). And this is a good thing. Grandmothers and grandfathers are our strength and our wisdom. May the Lord always give us wise elders! Elderly men and women who can pass on to us the memory of our people, the memory of the Church. May they also give us what the Letter to the Hebrews says about them: a sense of joy. It says that our forebears, our elders, greeted God's promises from afar. May this be what they teach us.

—ADDRESS TO THE CONVOCATION OF THE RENEWAL OF THE
HOLY SPIRIT, OLYMPIC STADIUM, JUNE 1, 2014

Bearing Fruit in Old Age

A people who does not take care of grandparents, who does not treat them well, has no future! Why does it have no future? Because such a people loses its memory and is torn from its roots. But beware: it is your responsibility to keep these roots alive in yourselves with prayer, by reading the Gospel, and with works of mercy. In this way we will remain as living trees, that even in old age will not stop bearing fruit. One of the most beautiful aspects of family life, of our human life as a family, is caressing a baby and being caressed by a grandfather and a grandmother.

ADDRESS AT A MEETING WITH THE ELDERLY,
ST. PETER'S SQUARE, SEPTEMBER 28, 2014

CHAPTER

8

THE CHURCH AS FAMILY

An Attentive Mama

The Church, in the fruitfulness of the Spirit, continues to generate new children in Christ, always listening to the Word of God and in docility to his plan of love. The Church is mother. The conception of Jesus in Mary's womb, in fact, is the prelude to the birth of every Christian in the womb of the Church. . . .

We understand, then, how the relationship which unites Mary and the Church is so deep: by looking at Mary, we discover the most beautiful and most tender face of the Church; and by looking at the Church, we recognize the sublime features of Mary. We Christians are not orphans, we have a mama, we have a mother, and this is great! We are not orphans! The Church is mother, Mary is mother.

The Church is our mother because she has given birth to us in Baptism. Each time we baptize a baby, he or she becomes a child of the Church, who enters the Church. And from that day, like an attentive mama, she helps us grow in faith and she shows us, with the strength of the Word of God, the path of salvation, defending us from harm. . . .

Dear friends, this is the Church, this is the Church we all love, this is the Church I love: a mother who has the good of her children at heart and who is able to give her life for them. We must not forget, however, that the Church is not only the priests, or we bishops; no, she is all of us! The Church is all of us! Agreed? And we, too, are children, but also mothers of other Christians. All who are baptized, men and women, together we are the Church. So often in our life we do not bear witness of this motherhood of the Church, of this maternal courage of the Church!

—GENERAL AUDIENCE,
ST. PETER'S SQUARE, SEPTEMBER 3, 2014

The Church Is Everyone's Home

In the family, everything that enables us to grow, to mature, and to live is given to each of us. We cannot grow up by ourselves; we cannot journey on our own, in isolation; rather, we journey and grow in a community, in a family. And so it is in the Church! In the Church we can listen to the word of God with the assurance that it is the message that the Lord has given us; in the Church we can encounter the Lord in the sacraments, which are the open windows through which the light of God is given to us, streams from which we can draw God's very life; in the Church we learn to live in the communion and love that comes from God.

Each one of us can ask himself or herself today: how do I live in the Church? When I go to church, is it as though I were at the stadium, at a football match? Is it as though I were at the cinema? No, it is something else. How do I go to church? How do I receive the gifts that the Church offers me to grow and mature as a Christian? Do I participate in the life of the community or do I go to church and withdraw into my own problems, isolating myself from others? In this first sense, the Church is catholic because she is everyone's home. Everyone is a child of the Church, and in her all find their home.

—GENERAL AUDIENCE,
ST. PETER'S SQUARE, OCTOBER 9, 2013

The Freedom to Say Yes

A good mother . . . helps [her children] to make definitive decisions with freedom. This is not easy, but a mother knows how to do it. But what does freedom mean? It is certainly not doing whatever you want, allowing yourself to be dominated by the passions, to pass from one experience to another without discernment, to follow the fashions of the day; freedom does not mean, so to speak, throwing everything that you don't like out the window.

No, that is not freedom! Freedom is given to us so that we know how to make good decisions in life! Mary as a good mother teaches us to be, like her, capable of making definitive decisions; definitive choices, at this moment in a time controlled by, so to speak, a philosophy of the provisional. It is very difficult to make a lifetime commitment. And she helps us to make those definitive decisions in the full freedom with which she said "yes" to the plan God had for her life (cf. Luke 1:38).

—Address at the Recitation of the Rosary, Papal Basilica of St. Mary Major, May 4, 2013

Helping Her Children Grow Strong

A mother helps her children grow up and wants them to grow strong; that is why she teaches them not to be lazy—which can also derive from a certain kind of well-being; not to sink into a comfortable lifestyle, contenting oneself with possessions. The mother takes care that her children develop better, that they grow strong, capable of accepting responsibilities, of engaging in life, of striving for great ideals. The Gospel of St. Luke tells us that in the family of Nazareth, Jesus "grew and became strong, filled with wisdom; and the favor of God was upon him" (2:40). Our Lady does just this for us; she helps us to grow as human beings and in the faith, to be strong and never to fall into the temptation of being human beings and Christians in a superficial way, but to live responsibly, to strive ever higher.

—ADDRESS AT THE RECITATION OF THE ROSARY,
PAPAL BASILICA OF ST. MARY MAJOR, 2013

Our Lady Hurries to Us

Our Lady, as soon as she had heard the news that she was to be the Mother of Jesus and the announcement that her cousin Elizabeth was expecting a child—the Gospel says—she went to her in haste; she did not wait. She did not say, "But now I am with child; I must take care of my health. My cousin is bound to have friends who can care for her." Something stirred her and she "went with haste" to Elizabeth (Luke 1:39). It is beautiful to think this of Our Lady, of our Mother, that she hastens because she intends to help. She goes to help; she doesn't go to boast and tell her cousin, "Listen, I'm in charge now, because I am the Mother of God!" No, she did not do that. She went to help! And Our Lady is always like this. She is our Mother who always hurries to us whenever we are in need.

—Homily, Saints Elizabeth and Zachariah Parish, Rome, May 26, 2013

We Belong to One Family

What is God's plan? It is to make of us all a single family of his children, in which each person feels that God is close and feels loved by him; as in the Gospel parable [of the prodigal son], feels the warmth of being God's family. The Church is rooted in this great plan. She is not an organization established by an agreement between a few people, but—as Pope Benedict XVI has so often reminded us—she is a work of God, born precisely from this loving design which is gradually brought about in history. The Church is born from God's wish to call all people to communion with him, to friendship with him; indeed, to share in his own divine life as his sons and daughters. The very word "church," from the Greek *ekklesia,* means "convocation": God convokes us, he impels us to come out of our individualism, from our tendency to close ourselves into ourselves, and he calls us to belong to his family.

—GENERAL AUDIENCE,
ST. PETER'S SQUARE, MAY 29, 2013

Mary's Motherhood Embraces Each of Us

Mary's faith is the fulfillment of Israel's faith, the whole journey, the whole path of that people awaiting redemption is contained in her, and it is in this sense that she is the model of the Church's faith, which has Christ, the incarnation of God's infinite love, as its center.

How did Mary live this faith? She lived it out in the simplicity of the thousand daily tasks and worries of every mother, such as providing food, clothing, caring for the house. . . . It was precisely Our Lady's normal life which served as the basis for the unique relationship and profound dialogue which unfolded between her and God, between her and her Son. Mary's "yes," already perfect from the start, grew until the hour of the cross. There her motherhood opened to embrace every one of us, our lives, so as to guide us to her Son. Mary lived perpetually immersed in the mystery of

God-made-man, as his first and perfect disciple, by contemplating all things in her heart in the light of the Holy Spirit, in order to understand and live out the will of God.

—GENERAL AUDIENCE,
ST. PETER'S SQUARE, OCTOBER 23, 2013

Our Lady in the Family

Let us think of Our Lady: Our Lady creates something in the Church that priests, bishops, and popes cannot create. She is the authentic feminine genius. And let us think about Our Lady in the families—about what Our Lady does in a family. It is clear that the presence of a woman in the domestic sphere is more necessary than ever, indeed, for the transmission of sound moral principles and for the transmission of the faith itself to future generations.

—ADDRESS TO THE NATIONAL CONGRESS OF THE ITALIAN WOMEN'S CENTER, CLEMENTINE HALL, JANUARY 25, 2014

Other Pope Francis Titles from

**Pope Francis Speaks
to Our Hearts**
192 pages, $10.95
Item# BPF1E3

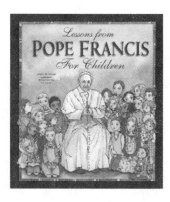

**Lessons from Pope Francis
for Children**
Hardcover, 32 pages, $12.95
Item# BCFRE5
For ages 7 to 11.

Available in the U.S. and
Canada only.

The Word Among Us Press

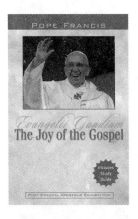

The Joy of the Gospel
Evangelii Gaudium
224 pages, $11.95
Item# BPFJE3

Includes Study Guide!

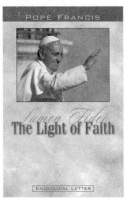

The Light of Faith
Lumen Fidei
88 pages, $8.95
Item# BPF2E3

the WORD among us®
The Spirit of Catholic Living

This book was published by The Word Among Us. Since 1981, The Word Among Us has been answering the call of the Second Vatican Council to help Catholic laypeople encounter Christ in the Scriptures.

The name of our company comes from the prologue to the Gospel of John and reflects the vision and purpose of all of our publications: to be an instrument of the Spirit, whose desire is to manifest Jesus' presence in and to the children of God. In this way, we hope to contribute to the Church's ongoing mission of proclaiming the gospel to the world so that all people would know the love and mercy of our Lord and grow ever more deeply in love with him.

Our monthly devotional magazine, *The Word Among Us*, features meditations on the daily and Sunday Mass readings, and currently reaches more than one million Catholics in North America and another half million Catholics in one hundred countries around the world. Our book division, The Word Among Us Press, publishes numerous books, Bible studies, and pamphlets that help Catholics grow in their faith.

To learn more about who we are and what we publish, log on to our website at www.wau.org. There you will find a variety of Catholic resources that will help you grow in your faith.

Embrace His Word, Listen to God . . .
www.wau.org